THE BATTERY BOOK

500 Ways to Charge Yourself Up

Joey Reiman

LONGSTREET PRESS
Atlanta, Georgia

Published by
LONGSTREET PRESS, INC.,
A Subsidiary of Cox Newspapers,
A Division of Cox Enterprises, Inc.
2140 Newmarket Parkway
Suite 118
Marietta, Georgia 30067

Printed in the United States of America

1st printing, 1993

Library of Congress Catalog Number 93-79668

ISBN: 1-56352-106-7

This book was printed by Data Reproductions Corporation, Rochester Hills, Michigan.

Cover design by Ian Berry
Cover photograph by Joe Boris
Book design and typesetting by Laura McDonald

— INTRODUCTION —

Life is electric when you're plugged into it. Energy abounds, creativity surges and the world lights up. You are positively charged!

Eventually, though, our batteries run down. It usually happens when we're bored, upset or just plain out of energy. As you know, the feeling ranges from bushed to beaten. The good news is that this is the very time we can learn how to recharge and renew ourselves, because in these moments are opportunities for us to create new sources of energy and exciting new ways to lift off, again. Unlike gravity, what goes down must go up.

In my first book, *Success: The Original Hand Book*, I tried to give people a hand by recounting the story of how my hand was paralyzed in an automobile accident and 100 percent revitalized by living a *thumbs-up* philosophy. As a motivational speaker, I shared my Hand Book with thousands of individuals throughout the country. I have witnessed people charging themselves up and revitalizing their spirits and hope.

The Battery Book encapsulates these travels and my personal experiences into a battery of easy-to-remember exercises and ideas. They have been designed to motivate you to take action, charge you up and get your juices going. When I started my advertising agency, I had no money, no office and lots of people saying "no way." Over the past eight years, the agency has become one of America's most prestigious firms. All because I kept going and going and going. You can do the same! Walt Disney went to 301 banks before number 302 bought what others called "a Mickey Mouse idea."

My favorite story is about a man whose batteries never wore down. First his business failed when he was 31. Then he ran for the state legislature at 33 and lost. He tried business again at 33 and failed, lost his fiancée to illness at 35, had a nervous breakdown at 36, ran again for Congress at 40 and was defeated. Again at 48 he ran and lost. At 55 he ran for the Senate and was defeated. He then lost a bid at the vice presidency at 56, and at 58, ran for the Senate and lost, again. This man ran and ran but he never ran out of hope. He elected to keep going. And at the age of 60, America elected Abraham Lincoln president.

All of us need our batteries charged up now and then. The results are immediate: we work better, we feel better and we look better. When the batteries in a flashlight are charged, the light shines brighter and you can see more. Your batteries work the same way. When they are charged, the world looks a whole lot brighter, too.

Beyond this page you'll find 500 different ways to recharge. They have all been tested and work! And unlike most batteries you buy in a store, they won't run out on you.

Ready to get plugged in?

Okay, charge!

THE
BATTERY BOOK

1. Remember, your birthday is God's lucky day.

2. The only risk in life is not taking one. Take one *now*!

3. Don't take the day off. Take the day on.

4. Life is not a dress rehearsal. It's time to act!

5. Write your goal on a small card. Now laminate it. Keep this card next to your driver's license so you'll never forget where you're going.

6.   Buy a piece of plush red carpet and put it beside your bed. Every morning when you get up, step on it and you'll be reminded of the treatment you deserve today.

7.   Take up gardening. You'll get exercise, breathe in fresh air and create life, and if you're lucky, your new hobby will grow on you.

8.   Take your favorite outfit out of your closet. Give away the remainder of your clothes to your favorite charity. Then start again. This time buy only favorite outfits.

9. Stop comparing yourself to others. Judging yourself this way causes 99 percent of life's misery.

10. Don't "should" on yourself. Remove the word from your vocabulary.

11. If God isn't near, you moved. Get closer by taking a quiet walk.

12. Plug into faith. It's your invisible means of support.

13. Hate people and you become their slave. Love them and you become their commander.

14. Be nice to everyone until 10:00 A.M. The rest of the day will take care of itself.

15. Sing *outside* the shower, too.

16. If you keep one foot in the past and one foot in the future, you end up tinkling on the present.

17. Don't seek a profession. Seek a passion.

18. Give a needy person five dollars. It will make you feel like a million.

19. Hug a tree. For centuries Native Americans have believed that trees possess amazing energy. Tap into it!

20. When in doubt, reach out.

21. J. Paul Getty and you both are worth 700,000. That's the average amount of hours everyone has to live. Invest them in yourself!

22. Take a trip anywhere.

23. Remember the word *inspire* means to breathe. So take a deep breath and hold it for a count of 3. Exhale at a count of 8. *Three-eight* rhymes with *create*.

24. Don't act like a mouse or the cat will eat you.

25. If you want to talk to God, pray. If you want to listen to God, meditate.

26. Replace T.G.I.F. with T.G.I.M.

27. Smile. Everyone loves you. They are just too shy to tell you.

28. The best present you can give yourself is the present.

29. Shoot for the stars. The worst that will happen is you'll hit a planet.

30. Visit a miniature horse farm.

31. If there is evil around you, just turn it around. Now it spells *live*.

32. Buy a child a toy. Then buy one for yourself. The child within you also needs to play.

33. Find yourself a goal and you will have found one of the most beautiful places on earth.

34. Do yoga.

35. Accept who you are. Then, be okay with it.

36. Think back to the finest moment of your life. Now you know what "reality" really is. Make every day a reality!

37. Thank God for God.

38. Don't worry about the money you've spent. Would you rather have given it to a doctor?

39. The next time you're afraid of something, exchange the word *afraid* with the word *excited*. Your stomach will feel a whole lot better.

40. Here's an easy 5,000-step exercise to alleviate stress: walk a mile.

41. Instead of crying over spilled milk, go milk another cow.

42. Remember the sign on Ted Turner's desk: "Lead, follow, or get out of the way."

43. Don't test the waters, make waves.

44. Keep in mind that success is a marathon, not a sprint.

45. Always live your life on purpose.

46. Get a massage and your spirit will get the message.

47. Tell a friend a secret.

48. Laugh until you just about cry.

49. Dance in your underwear.

50. Buy a new pair of shoes. Then go somewhere your old shoes have never been before.

51. Hug a friend and make sure you're the last to let go.

52. One deep breath fills your lungs with four times the oxygen they usually get and gives you a fresh sense of well-being.

53. Don't take life so seriously. You won't get out alive.

54. Have yourself paged at an airport or train station. It always feels good to hear your name.

55. Buy a newspaper and a cup of coffee and browse the world you live in. Read all the good news you can find.

56. Play the harmonica. It will help you control your breathing and get you in tune with yourself.

57. Give your mind a positive charge every morning by thinking a positive thought.

58. Think about love.

59. Keep a diary of everything you're doing right. Fill it up.

60. Send a card to someone who needs a kind word.

61. Test drive the car of your dreams.

62. Imagine you have all that you want and try to be nice to others.

63. Buy a down comforter.

64. Travel home a different way.

65. Remember that you generate your own electricity. You don't need to get a charge from anyone but yourself.

66. Avoid circuit overload. Instead of trying to move the boulder, break it into pebbles. Before you know it, you've moved mountains.

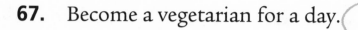
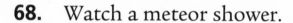
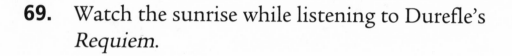

67. Become a vegetarian for a day.

68. Watch a meteor shower.

69. Watch the sunrise while listening to Durefle's *Requiem*.

70. Invite 5 people who can't say enough good things about you to dinner. Then just sit and listen.

71. Winning ideas that stay in our heads are losers. Act on the one that's on top of your mind, now!

72. Go to an art gallery. Soak up the local color.

73. Never forget that your goal in life is to wake up excited and go to bed feeling safe.

74. Bake a cake. Then eat it.

75. Go to a clothing store with a friend and tell her that you want to buy something for your best friend. Ask her to help you pick it out. When she does, have it gift-wrapped and give it to her.

76. Go to the park and swing.

77. Get a foot massage from a reflexologist and you'll be able to conquer any "feat" in the world. The Egyptian kings and queens claimed it was the best way to recharge.

78. Take a pottery class. You'll find that the vessel you create will hold a lot more for you than just paper clips.

79. Buy yourself at least 200-count, 100 percent cotton sheets and go to sleep early. Give yourself a rest.

80. If you're having trouble believing, *make believe* and you will.

81. Forget your A.B.C.'s and remember your C.B.A.'s: Conceiving, Believing and Achieving.

82. Send yourself 11 roses with a note that says, You're 12.

83. The greatest pleasure in life is doing exactly what you think you can't do.

84. Think of the word *enemy* as short for *end-of-me*.

85. Believe, and unbelievable things will happen.

86. Listen to the soundtrack of *Pippin*.

87. Watch the movie *Enchanted Cottage*, a magical film in which ugliness turns to beauty when two people turn to love.

88. Act—don't react.

89. Take the day off and spend time working on yourself.

90. If you want to bear delicious fruit, you've got to be planted on good ground.

91. To insure initial success, remember what your initials stand for:

A — Action	J — Joyous	S — Safe
B — Believer	K — Knowledgeable	T — Truth
C — Confident	L — Loving	U — Unique
D — Dauntless	M — Merry	V — Valuable
E — Exciting	N — Now	W — Winner
F — Fearless	O — Optimist	X — Xmas
G — Giving	P — Perfect	Y — Yes
H — Happy	Q — Quality	Z — Zeal
I — Intelligent	R — Rich	

92. Put your thumb out and hitch a ride to nowhere. Put your thumb up to hitch a ride to the top.

93. Remember, life is not a charge card. It has no limits.

94. Party with positive people.

95. Ask yourself if you would still keep your job without a paycheck. If the answer is no, it's time to check out another job.

96. Become friendly with a restaurant owner. Chances are you'll never have to wait in line again.

97. Take a bubble bath.

98. Make yourself some comfort food. My top three choices are:

1. A cheese dream—the ultimate midnight snack. Take two pieces of bread, two slices of American cheese and two slices of tomato. Butter a skillet and place it on a burner on medium heat. Toast the bread on one side. Flip the toast and throw on the cheese

and tomatoes. Then put them all together and
press the sandwich into the skillet. Yum.

2. Pasta with garlic to immunize your body from colds.
3. Bow-tie pasta with a 1/2 cup of cottage cheese and
   1/2 cup of sour cream.

99. Watch a sunrise. It proves that darkness never
lasts. In fact, the darkest part of the night
lasts only one hour.

100. Take a walk on the beach. You'll notice the
ocean always waves hello.

101. Go to a maternity ward. You'll see a glimpse
of the future, and baby it'll make you feel great.

102. Ask any musician. The hardest part of practicing is opening the case. Open it now!

103. Exorcise the bad by exercising good.

104. Have a glass of Ovaltine.

105. Subtract the ads. The average American will see 21,000 T.V. commercials a year. Most of them will tell you what to wear, where to go and whom to admire. Many ads add up to nothing. Remember, there are only four products in the world: Baking soda, alcohol, jeans and tires. Everything else is made out of them. Just be yourself. After all, there's only one *real thing* — YOU!

106. Listen to *An English Ladymass*, by Anonymous 4. It's an incredibly beautiful collection of thirteenth- and fourteenth-century chants; available on CD.

107. If someone yells at you, he is screaming for help. Remember, he is a lot more afraid than you are.

108. Stop smoking by picking a day that's important to you. On December 4, my father died and so did my desire to join him. I haven't smoked since.

109. Laughter is the most powerful state of mind there is. When you're laughing you can't think of anything else. *Laugh.*

110. Branch out to your relatives by starting a family tree.

111. Take a set of bed sheets and sprinkle a bit of talcum powder on them. Then make your bed. Pleasant dreams.

112. Do you have a dream that others would call a Mickey Mouse idea? That's what 301 banks called Walt Disney's idea. He finally sold his theme park concept to number 302. Start building your Disneyland today.

113. Wear red shoes. You'll stop people in their tracks and you'll feel like dancing.

114. The Red Sea parted *only* when Moses put his foot in the water. Take the first step now.

115. Jesus said, "Seek and you shall find." Listen to him.

116. Follow Confucius, who said, "All great journeys begin with one step."

117. If you want to *clean up*, just dust off your dream.

118. Read the history of the land you live on.

119. Don't compete with anyone but yourself. Competition is for horses.

120. Listen to your favorite music.

121. Trying times are times for trying.

122. Have a cappuccino with sprinkled chocolate and extra whipped cream.

123. Next time you need someone to come to your rescue, you be the hero!

124. You want to feel six feet higher than you ever have before? Just take a walk through the nearest cemetery.

125. Go to an amusement park.

126. As Peter Pan pointed out, "Just think lovely thoughts and you'll go up! up! up!"

127. Have a glass of freshly squeezed orange juice. And remember this: when the orange was under lots of pressure, it produced the sweetest stuff in the world.

128. Ride a horse and you'll be galloping with energy long afterwards!

129. The outside of a pet is good for the inside of a person. Everyone ought to own at least one.

130. Try a face mask.

131. Have a slumber party.

132. Send a Valentine's Day card early.

133. Remember, good happens. Make it true for someone.

134. Leo F. Buscaglia on how he gets charged up: "It's easy for me to get charged up by simply remembering that we are all here on borrowed time. We don't have forever. Death is very dramatic . . . it comes to everyone, often unannounced and always final. I take up the challenge and tell myself, the time to live, love, change, experience, share, celebrate, appreciate, reciprocate . . . is NOW."

135. Face the sun and you'll find that the shadows fall only behind you.

136. Climb a mountain.

137. Want to be a hero? Do the thing you fear most.

138. Want a quick dose of happiness? Make someone else happy.

139. Go to a wedding. It's where angels hang out.

140. Every April you have the choice of what to think about—the showers coming down or the flowers coming up.

141. Be enthusiastic. The word comes from the Greek word for *inspired*. Fake it if you must, but be it.

142. Remember, rough seas make a great captain.

143. Lip sync your favorite song.

144. Never forget that the meaning of life is to live it.

145. Look for happiness right in your backyard.

146. Famous artist John Baldessari on how he gets charged up: "Have lots of ideas; throw away the bad ones."

147. Think like Samuel Goldwyn, who summed up his life in two words: I'm possible.

148. Look up to the stars; you'll soon realize how short a time we are here. By the time you see the light from the star, it no longer exists.

149. While others curse the darkness, light a candle.

150. Order a special meal on your next flight for a special person. YOU.

151. Go to the movies in the afternoon.

152. Take a picture of yourself when you're happy.

153. As Jiminy Cricket says, "Accentuate the positive and eliminate the negative."

154. Turn your idea into "I did it."

155. If you have employees who are not fired with enthusiasm, fire them with enthusiasm.

156. Remember, the difference between "outselling" and "out-selling" is a little dash.

157. Helen Gurley Brown on how she gets charged up: "Fear of failing, of not being able to 'get back in school,' and an hour and a half of exercise every day make it possible for me to get up and do it all over again the next day!"

158. Make yourself a cup of Ginseng tea.

159. Wash your hair with peppermint shampoo.

160. Sail. It will give you a second wind.

161. Learn a good joke.

162. Go to a party and send out positive signals. Don't be surprised to find the party centered around you.

163. Let someone tickle you.

164. Dance to music as if it were written just for you.

165. Baby yourself. It's a chance for you to be the parent you never had.

166. Collect wildflowers and give them to someone you're wild about.

167. Wash windows. Everything will look clearer.

168. Call someone you haven't spoken to for years.

169. Write the words *thank you* in the memo line on your checks. After all, aren't you thankful for electricity and gas and water?

170. Talk to your pillow at night about joy, happiness and confidence. You'll have better dreams.

171. Remember A.M. and P.M. stand for Action Moments and Peaceful Moments.

172. Volunteer to feed the homeless. You'll never feel so full.

173. Never give up. Paul Cézanne was rejected by Paris' leading art school five times because they said he didn't have much style.

174. If you want your dreams to happen, wake up!

175. Make sure your batteries have plenty of juice by having a good healthy breakfast.

176. If it bleeds, it leads. So be sure to skip the first part of the 11:00 news.

177. Write a poem.

178. Accept a compliment.

179. Read *The Velveteen Rabbit* by Margery Williams.

180. Never forget: there's only one "U" in this universe.

181. Join a cinema club so you can see movies before there're shown to the public.

182. Live in the fast lane and you'll have more accidents than those of us in the right lane who enjoy the ride and often get there sooner.

183. Stop worrying. If you think about getting burned, you'll never find your place in the sun.

184. If you want more out of life, put more into life.

185. Action always precedes motivation. Not the other way around.

186. Try asking yourself, "What would God do in this situation?" Then do it.

187. If you want to live in a prettier neighborhood, plant some flowers outside. If you want kinder neighbors, cut them a bouquet. If you want a more beautiful house, invite them in.

188. Good news: Your soul never runs out of energy!

189. The best way to lose weight is to gain more — more friends, more interests and more fun. Never, ever put life on a diet. You'll end up losing.

190. Get a daring haircut. It will put you on a new wave length.

191. Remember, you only get one chance to live your life. Even if you're reincarnated, it's hard to remember what you missed the first time.

192. Enthusiasm is your faith caught on fire.

193. Buy Shirley MacLaine's "Inner Workout" tape. It's a program for stress reduction and relaxation through meditation.

194. Give away money on your birthday as a celebration of your life.

195. Spend a day on a farm. Milk a cow.

196. Don't wait until the mood hits you. Do it now.

197. Kiss your mirror in the morning. It will reflect well on you throughout the day.

198. Success expects success.

199. You must focus on your target if you want to hit a bullseye.

200. Buy silk underwear for yourself.

201. Find a mentor.

202. Become a mentor.

203. Remember, one person with passion is a majority.

204. Keep this in mind: you are what you think.

205. St. Francis of Assisi on how to get charged up: "Grant that I may not so much seek to be consoled as to console. To be understood, as to understand. To be loved as to love. For it is in giving that we receive!"

206. Get excited about problems. They are just disguised opportunities.

207. Put a half spoonful of soil into a glass of water. Shake it up. See how cloudy it is? Now let it sit for an hour. Soon the water will clear as the soil sinks to the bottom. Your mind works the same way. Sit quietly for a while. See how clear it is?

208. Adopt a cause.

209. Remember, happiness isn't created. It's revealed.

210. Your immune system works better when you are happy. When you warm up to yourself, it is almost impossible to get a cold.

211. The dictionary is the only place where the word *achieve* comes before *believe*.

212. Think of the word *win* as an acronym for Whip Insecurity Now.

213. If you want an answer to a problem, go to sleep. Francis Scott Key just couldn't come up with the words for a song in his head. He went to sleep and dreamed "The Star Spangled Banner."

214. You have only have two kinds of worry. The first are things too little to worry about. The second are things you can't do anything about. So now you don't have a worry in the world.

215. Listen to Teddy Roosevelt: "Far better it is to dare mighty things, though checkered by failure, than to live in the gray twilight that knows not victory nor defeat."

216. Go to a Broadway musical.

217. Float in the ocean.

218. Take a hot bath.

219. Instead of asking who is right, ask what is right.

220. Recharge yourself every holiday.

221. New Year's: Don't just make resolutions, have a *new you* party where you celebrate you!

222. Valentine's Day: Send flowers to yourself.

223. March 4th: March forth and take action on your ideas.

224. March 15th: Martin Luther King, Jr., had a dream. Identify yours today to celebrate his birthday.

225. July 4th: Become independent. Remember, you don't need permission to follow your heart.

226. October 12th: Do what Columbus did. Discover something new about the world.

227. Halloween: Do something you've always been scared of doing. By midnight the fear should be gone.

228. November 4th: Vote for yourself on election day.

229. Thanksgiving: Thank everyone for giving you so much.

230. Chanukah: This is a time of great joy. Send out invitations that say, "Have N' Gala."

231. Christmas: Go to midnight Mass. It's been one of the most beautiful and spiritual events for centuries.

232. Don't stop. "The truest wisdom," Napoleon wrote, "is a resolute determination."

233. If you found out you only had a certain amount of time to live, how much would each minute be worth to you? Next time someone is late for an appointment, charge him.

234. Don't harbor hateful thoughts. Hate hurts you.

235. Buy new make-up.

236. If you compromise with someone, you both lose. If you negotiate, you both win.

237. When we feel hurt by someone, we have the real power. The power to forgive.

238. Paint a beautiful picture of yourself.

239. Live your life expecting a miracle every day.

240. Don't be afraid of taking a big leap. You can't cross a ravine in two small jumps.

241. Thoughts have wings. Clip the negative ones.

242. Never let a day end being angry at someone. It saps your energy.

243. Don't be afraid of the dark. Remember, we need the night to see the stars.

244. When your car battery is low and someone gives you a jump, your car is recharged. People work the same way. Have you given someone a jump today?

245. Repeat this affirmation: I am charged with all the energy the world has created. I now can create anything.

246. Make a trans-Atlantic crossing by boat. There's nothing in the world quite as energizing as seeing land when you haven't for a week.

247. Go to your favorite place to re-energize.

248. Replace your batteries at a day spa.

249. Sit under a big, big, big tree.

250. Discover your very own island. Try the Bahamas. They have nearly 700, nearby.

251. Marinate in positive thought as you float in your bathtub.

252. Count your blessings while sitting under the stars. They should add up to the same number.

253. Breathe in the air atop a mountain.

254. Go fishing. You're bound to catch lots of positive energy.

255. Re-energize atop the Statue of Liberty.

256. Sit quietly at the bottom of the Lincoln Memorial.

257. Savor a moment in the arms of a loved one.

258. Make a milkshake and taste how sweet life is.

259. Never talk about limitations. Even "the sky's the limit" is negative. No one has ever found a limit for human beings. So unlimit yourself.

260. Give someone a thumbs-up. See what you get back.

261. Remember, the sweet smell of success is always right under your nose.

262. Ask your loved one to applaud you once a day. You do the same. There's nothing quite like the sound or the feeling.

263. Write the word *limit* on a piece of toilet paper and flush it down the john.

264. Do any chore. Once it's done, you'll feel accomplished.

265. Don't tiptoe to your grave. Dance.

266. Keep your plan to yourself. After all, life is like a picture — if you overexpose it, it won't come out.

267. Have a cup of spearmint tea.

268. The famous Yogi Ramachakra stored up new energy by placing his feet together and locking the fingers of both hands. This closed the circuit. Then he breathed rhythmically a few times and was recharged.

269. Create anything. It's intelligence having fun.

270. Watch a funny movie.

271. If you're alone, take yourself to dinner.

272. Instead of giving your children a "no!," give them a "go."

273. Create a life-long romance with yourself.

274. Remember, you don't need permission to feel good.

275. Always be ready for more money.

276. Play in the rain (naked, if you wish), and let it wash away all your fears.

277. Next time you get a cold, enjoy it. Your body is telling you to take a break before *it* breaks, so make some soup or order out. Watch a great movie and just lie around in comfy pajamas or an old favorite t-shirt. Your body will appreciate this vacation. Like you, it doesn't like to work when the temperature hits 100.

278. Your past is not your life. It's history.

279. Go out and have a picnic.

280. Eat an apple dipped in honey.

281. Write a letter to the author of your favorite book.

282. Be the live wire of the party!

283. Live your dreams, not someone else's.

284. You can play any part in life you want. Ronald Reagan lost the role of a U.S. president in the 1964 film *The Best Man* because he didn't look the part. He certainly showed them.

285. Peace of mind is knowing who you are and knowing you're okay.

286. Ask a child who God is.

287. Save a bird's life. It may have flown into a window or been hit by a car. Nurse it back to health and you'll be flying high.

288. Remember, a clenched fist cannot shake hands.

289. The best revenge is moving forward. Move!

290. The best ideas are in graveyards buried with the people who had them. Only action will keep ideas alive.

291. Be in awe of yourself.

292. The definition of power is the *ability* to act.

293. Abraham Lincoln recharged by believing this: "Always bear in mind that your own resolution to success is more important than any one thing."

294. Think of yourself as a Federal Express package and your goal as something that *absolutely, positively has to be there.*

295. Go to a parade. Make believe it's for you.

296. Go white-water rafting.

297. Should someone tell you to "go fly a kite," don't be discouraged. Just remember Ben Franklin "lit up" at the idea.

298. If there isn't a good job where you live, move.

299. Ray Kroc, founder of McDonald's, kept his batteries charged by remembering, "When you're green, you grow; when you're ripe, you rot."

300. NIKE says, "Just Do It." But only you can say, "Just Did It."

301. Go whale watching. They are related to humans, so they'll be watching you, too.

302. Close your eyes. What you see is called insight.

303. Remember, the word *won* has the word *now* in it!

304. Watercolors will help you paint a better picture of the world you live in. Buy a set and carry it with you.

305. Take an afternoon nap.

306. There's no such thing as dividing up the pie. So don't divide up the pie; bake a cake. Life is a bakery, full of sweets.

307. Hold a pen with your teeth. This activates the smiling muscles.

308. Talk to your grandparents about anything.

309. Help save a rain forest. Of the 3,000 plants identified by the National Cancer Institute as offering potential cures for cancer, 70 percent are located in there.

310. Have breakfast in bed.

311. Choose a fragrance for yourself. The famous choreographer Ballanchine chose different perfumes for his dancers. He figured if they were as light as air, he should be able to sense their presence.

312. Challenge yourself to be yourself.

313. Eat a piece of chocolate.

314. Atlanta's Mayor Maynard Jackson charges himself up by remembering what his Dad always said: "When best is better, good is not good enough."

315. It's nice to be important, but it's more important to be nice.

316. Tell a child she's great at something. Be specific.

317. Moses, Muhammad and Buddha found great inspiration in contemplative silence. Quiet, you'll like it.

318. Change your daily routine.

319. Read the Bible.

320. Remember, there's no doubt in clout.

321. President Clinton has helped make hugging acceptable among men. Whether you voted for him or not, this is one practice you might want to elect.

322. Memorize this charge: If it is to be, it is up to me.

323. When it comes to buying securities, invest in "I" stock.

324. Don't forget that fireflies light up only when they are moving forward.

325. Stick your neck out. Giraffes have endured while other animals did not because they were constantly reaching up for their food. And guess what? They have the same amount of neck bones as we do.

326. Remember, "healthy self" really spells "heal-thy self."

327. The next time you feel bad about getting old, remember that many are denied the privilege.

328. Tell everyone you care about that you love them.

329. If you want to get to happiness, just make a right.

330. Clean up a room. You'll see and feel the results immediately.

331. Arthur Cohen, Ph.D., and dear friend, says, "If you're the boss and you treat me like nothing, then you're the boss of nothing."

332. Contribute more and you shall receive more. If you want a stronger rebound, throw the ball harder.

333. Hardening of the heart ages people faster than hardening of the arteries.

334. If you're flat on your back, there is no way to look but up.

335. Remember this if you're angry: the fire department never fights fire with fire.

336. Being stranded at third base adds no more to the game than striking out.

337. Remember, the day which we fear is our last is but the birthday of our eternity.

338. Keep the holiday spirit in your heart and you will also find it right at your door. Santa doesn't enter through the chimney. He enters through the heart.

339. It's not so much what you are eating, it's what's eating you.

340. Give a kind thought. It has more value than a material gift because it cannot be bought.

341. Reaching high keeps you on your toes.

342. Always remember that anger is one letter short of danger.

343. Look back and it's always depressing. If it was good, it's gone and if it was bad, who needs it? Always look ahead. It's where hope lives and waits for you.

344. Have a glass of cold spring water with a lemon in it.

345. Take an exhilarating dip in a cool stream.

346. Change the way people think of you by changing what you think of yourself.

347. Remember, the harder you work the luckier you will get.

348. Take a child to the zoo for the first time.

349. Look outside yourself for happiness and dream. Or look inside, and awake!

350. Remember, you are God-like because you create your own world.

351. Buy a plant and grow with it. Every time you give it water, give yourself something to quench your thirst for life. And make sure it has lots of sun. Remember, light makes plants grow and enlightenment makes humans grow.

352. Make a sign that says "yes."

353. Buy a box of crayons and put them in your desk at work.

354. Compliment yourself.

355. Walk around with a smile on your face as if you are the owner of a wonderful secret.

356. Go to the library.

357. Make the world your home. Write to foreign embassies for travel posters and international stores for their catalogs.

358. Think about the person you like the most.

359. Play an electric guitar.

360. Take a trip on a train.

361. Buy yourself some expensive soap.

362. Call your Mom. After all, if you turn the word upside down, it spells WOW.

363. Become a possibilitarian!

364. Don't worry. The darkest hour is only 60 minutes long.

365. The only liability in life is not living it.

366. Buy a star. That's right—you can own one by writing to the International Star Register.

367. Watch the movie *E.T.* again.

368. Make sure the ladder you're climbing is leaning on your own house.

369. Remember Henry Ford's words: "Whether you think you can or you think you can't, you are right."

370. Help the environment by clearing the air with friends and family.

371. Sow kindness this season, and next season you'll reap a crop of friends.

372. Remember, the best you can do is your most.

373. If you want to hit the jackpot, you have to put the coin in the machine.

374. Make this toast: May everything you wish for be the least you get.

375. Go into your backyard or nearby park and name as many trees as you can. Then visit them as often as possible.

376. Remember, if you want the fruit, you have to go out on the limb.

377. Passion is the electricity of life. Make sure you never run out of it.

378. Run through the sprinkler on a hot summer day.

379. Get your body in tone by getting your mind in tune.

380. *Push up* your expectations of success.

381. *Jump* over your worries.

382. *Run* through your perfect day in your mind.

383. *Lift* the weight of the world off your shoulders.

384. *Stretch* your imagination.

385. *Reach* up to the sky.

386. *Breathe* in the fresh possibilities.

387. Follow the words of Epictetus: Learn to wish that everything should come to pass exactly as it does.

388. Kiss a baby.

389. Throw a snowball.

390. Buy some play-dough and take a whiff. It will bring back fun memories.

391. Go to Radio City Music Hall.

392. Learn how to waltz to the "Blue Danube." You'll feel like a prince and princess.

393. It takes 43 muscles to frown and 15 to smile. Save energy and smile.

394. When you're in a good mood, so is the world.

395. Remember, misery may love company, but company doesn't love misery.

396. Pick your favorite star in the night sky. Now remember the reason it's there is to remind you of why there is a heaven. As Robert Browning put it, "Ah, but a man's reach should exceed his grasp. Or what's a heaven for?"

397. If you think your relationship doesn't have a prayer, reignite it by praying together. Studies prove that couples who pray together stay together.

398. Be outgoing and wonderful things will be incoming.

399. Take a lesson from angels. They can fly because they take themselves lightly.

400. Successful people think about success.

401. When a thought says no, just tell it to go.

402. It wasn't the spinach that kept Popeye strong, it was his attitude — "I Yam what I Yam."

403. The best ship to brave the waves is a friendship.

404. Read *SUCCESS: The Original Hand Book* by me. In it you'll find that life's five greatest secrets are right in your hand!

— Your *thumb* reminds you to be "thumbs-up."
— Your *pointer* reminds you to point at your goal.
— Your *middle finger* goes to fear.
— Your *fourth finger* reminds you to go forth and take action on your ideas.
— Your *little finger* reminds you that God is in the details and the little things in life — like a flower, a smile and a thank you — can change your whole world or someone else's.

405. Treat yourself to a retreat. After all, the best must rest.

406. You can wait a long, long time to obtain wisdom or you can spend a short time with anyone over 75. Older people are the pearls.

407. Clear your fog with a 30-minute jog.

408. If you want to improve your love life, love life.

409. Remember that when you blow a fuse your power shuts off.

410. Take a bicycle ride.

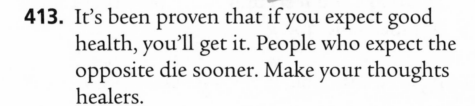

411. Say no.

412. Smell a rose.

413. It's been proven that if you expect good health, you'll get it. People who expect the opposite die sooner. Make your thoughts healers.

414. Give someone hope. It's something they will keep forever.

415. Listen to music by John Williams. He'll put your head in the stars where it belongs.

416. Eat chili peppers. Studies suggest they help prevent heart attacks, prevent some cancers, burn up excess calories, break up congestion and make you feel euphoric. How's that for a hot medicine tip?

417. If you want to be happy, just be.

418. Have pride in your home.

419. Spend *quantity* time with your children.

420. Make a new friend.

421. Watch a lightning storm (but watch out).

422. Dine out.

423. Get enough sleep.

424. Get your holiday shopping done before you get wrapped up in the holiday.

425. When someone asks you, "How are you?" reply, "Perfect." After all, you are.

426. Remember, the best way to keep your family charged up is to all stay connected.

427. Invest in another's happiness and the return will be unlimited funs.

428. If you don't know what to "go for" in life, go fishing. You're bound to catch some big ideas.

429. Never lose in your imagination.

430. Remember, the greatest things in life are not things.

431. Children who are good natured have been good nurtured. Hug them the next time you see them.

432. Never say I don't know. You are all knowing.

433. Put ten dollars away every month for a year. Then take yourself to a fabulous charity ball. And don't forget that the ticket is also a tax deduction.

434. Happiness is thinking it.

435. Envy no one. Count your blessings, not theirs.

436. Improve the environment by keeping your mind clear of garbage.

437. Adopt an angel.

438. Buy a toy for your bathtub.

439. Start a butterfly farm or visit one. It's a beautiful opportunity to see what heaven is for someone who had to crawl through life.

440. Never "face the facts" because they are often not the truth. Fifty years ago the "fact" was that polio could not be cured. So much for the facts.

441. Listen to your heart. It's poetic.

442. Put an upbeat message on your answering machine like, "This machine records only good news."

443. Winston Churchill believed, "The empires of the future are the empires of the mind."

444. When you get down, remember life is too short for a long face.

445. Your thoughts are magnets.

446. Buy a juicer. Buy some fruit. Congratulations. You've just bought yourself health. My favorite is mixing 1/2 cup of strawberries, 1/2 a banana and 1 orange. Be sure to squeeze a glass into your schedule.

447. Beware of negative elevator people. They hang out in elevators and say discouraging things like, "Two days until Friday," "Oh no, another day," and "I should have stayed in bed today."

448. Norman Vincent Peale said it all with, "Throw your heart over the fence and the rest of your body will follow."

449. Read yourself a children's book. It will make you feel like a child. Here are some of my favorites:

The Giving Tree, by Shel Silverstein
Goodnight Moon, by Marcia Brown
The Little Train That Could, by Walter Piper

450. Celebrate Marconi's birthday (he invented the battery). April 25.

451. Walk tall.

452. Repeat the words of Helen Keller to yourself: "Life is either a daring adventure or nothing at all."

453. Ride a roller coaster. It's a 2-minute version of life.

454. If you live in New York City, move.

455. Build a sand castle.

456. Have your astrological chart done.

457. Laugh. Humor heals.

458. When you're scared, pretend to be brave.

459. Find a beautiful frame. Put a picture of yourself in it.

460. Stop all communication with people who make you feel bad.

461. Take more pictures. They make the past a present.

462. Adopt an animal from the pound. You'll be helping two lives.

463. Go to a waterfall, a babbling brook or a fountain and listen to the sound of moving water. It will give your spirit a fabulous shower.

464. Play the theme from *Rocky*. It will help you have a knock-out day!

465. Should you get down, don't dismay. The sun goes down every day, too, but comes back up the next.

466. Think of the whole world as your friend.

467. Not choosing is a choice you never want to make. Choose and you'll never lose.

468. Attract bigger things by thinking bigger thoughts.

469. Take your mind jogging by thinking of all the beauty around you. Do this for five minutes and I promise you'll feel better all day long.

470. If you don't want to take your worries to heart, get them off your chest by sharing them.

471. Learn something new you've always wanted to do.

472. Teach a child how to fly a kite.

473. Galileo would never have seen the light if he went to bed before dark.

474. Take a cooking class.

475. Have a dress or suit custom-made for you. Just buy one off the rack and change its buttons. Now your outfit is a one-of-a-kind.

476. Let go.

477. Welcome dissatisfaction because it will always lead you to action.

478. Go up in a hot air balloon.

479. Go to the opera. The climactic movement will feel like a thousand volts.

480. Listen to anything by Wagner.

481. Watch a child smell a flower for the first time.

482. Stretch once a day. It relieves tight muscles, reduces stress and creates vitality. A good stretch to the sky will also keep you on your toes.

483. Recent studies reveal that meditation keeps you young. Perhaps sitting cross-legged a few minutes a day is something to ponder.

484. Make up a children's story. Then tell it to a child.

485. Make a tape with your own voice telling yourself what you want out of life. Play it back once a week.

486. Forgive yourself and you will heal yourself.

487. Remember that the road is always better than the inn.

488. Buy a teddy bear for yourself. Give it a name.

489. Whistle.

490. Go antique shopping. Appreciating the old will always make you feel young.

491. Play your stereo loud.

492. Dr. Louis Pasteur never would have gotten his shot if he hadn't kept going.

493. Watch cartoons and watch yourself smile.

494. Go to the cemetery to visit someone you love. After all, cemeteries are for the living.

495. According to a recent study, every mile a sedentary person walks or runs adds 21 minutes to his life.

496. Think about friendship.

497. Clean out a closet. It will help clear your mind.

498. You can't step in the same river twice. Accept change and go with the flow.

499. List ten things that charge you up personally. Write them down in this book.

500. Reread this book.